A Noble French Patriot

by Alexandra King

 HOUGHTON MIFFLIN HARCOURT
School Publishers

PHOTOGRAPHY CREDITS: **Cover** Private Collection, Peter Newark American Pictures/The Bridgeman Art Library. **Title page** © Time Life Pictures/Mansell/Time Life Pictures/Getty Images. **4** © Time Life Pictures/Mansell/Time Life Pictures/Getty Images. **6** Private Collection, Peter Newark American Pictures/The Bridgeman Art Library. **10** © CORBIS. **11** © The Granger Collection, New York. **13** Library of Congress, LC-DIG-pga-01591. **14** © CORBIS. **16** © Erich Lessing/Art Resource, NY.

Printed in China

ISBN-13: 978-0-547-01665-8
ISBN-10: 0-547-01665-4

6 7 8 9 0940 18 17 16 15 14 13
4500396626

Table of Contents

Introduction

To Patriot troops during the American Revolution, he was "the soldier's friend." To Americans everywhere, he was "our Marquis" (mar KEE). To the founders and first presidents of the United States, he was a personal friend. George Washington loved him like a son. His contributions both in American battles and at the royal court in France helped America win its independence from the British.

Who was he? He was Gilbert du Motier, the Marquis de Lafayette, a French nobleman who became a hero of the Revolutionary War.

Lafayette's Early Life

Lafayette was born September 6, 1757, in Auvergne, France, into a prominent aristocratic family. When Lafayette was not quite two years old, his father was killed during a battle against France's longtime enemy, Great Britain.

Lafayette's mother brought him to Paris, the French capital, when he was 11. She knew he needed to be exposed to the manners of the French royal court in order to succeed. The young boy was enrolled in a school for sons of the aristocracy, where his class-mates were future dukes, counts, and kings of France.

Within a year of his arrival in Paris, Lafayette's mother and grandfather passed away. Lafayette inherited the noble title *marquis* and his family's vast wealth. As a result, he became one of the richest noblemen in France.

Lafayette's marriage to Adrienne de Noailles, the daughter of another wealthy noble family, took place in 1774 when the marquis was 16. Around the same time, he undertook military officer's training and, at age 18, became a captain in the horse-mounted infantry. The young Lafayette dreamed of achieving glory in battle against the British.

A Far-Off Revolution

Meanwhile, thousands of miles away across the Atlantic Ocean, the Revolutionary War had begun. Word of the American colonists' revolt against Britain soon reached France.

Many French military officers, including Lafayette, were impressed by the Patriots' readiness to fight for freedom from British bondage. Some French officers even traveled to America to fight for the colonists' cause. Lafayette also greatly admired the ideas of liberty and equality that the American revolutionaries supported.

Lafayette's imagination blazed with thoughts of helping the colonists in their fight against the British. "I gave my heart to the Americans and thought of nothing else," he wrote.

A portrait of the Marquis de Lafayette

Burning with eagerness, the 19-year-old Lafayette arranged to meet with Silas Deane, an American diplomat who was in Paris. Lafayette had a bold request. He asked Deane to make him a general in the American army.

Deane was tentative at first because Lafayette had no actual battle experience. To persuade the diplomat, Lafayette emphasized his passion for the American cause, his wealth, and his powerful connections. Finally, Deane agreed.

When the French king, Louis XVI, heard of the marquis's plan, he opposed it. He thought that a French nobleman serving as an American general would be a political disaster for the French government.

At this time, Great Britain and France were at peace. The king feared that the presence of a prominent French aristocrat such as Lafayette fighting on behalf of American colonists would send an antagonistic message to the British government. Lafayette's actions could even lead to war between France and Great Britain—something that Louis XVI wanted very much to avoid.

But Lafayette was determined to go to America and fight for the colonists' freedom. He bought his own ship and defiantly planned to go to America, with or without the king's blessing.

After a dramatic series of events, including a decoy trip to London, threats of imprisonment by Louis XVI, and a chase across France on horseback, Lafayette finally got his wish. He sailed for the American colonies on April 20, 1777.

Lafayette meets General George Washington for the first time.

Meeting General Washington

Two months later, Lafayette's ship landed near Charleston, South Carolina. Upon arrival, Lafayette and his band of French officers set out for Philadelphia to present themselves to Congress. It was a grueling trip; they traveled by foot through rough terrain and exhausting heat. Some of them fell ill, but Lafayette grew more excited and optimistic with every step northward.

Lafayette felt entirely at home in America. In particular, the simpler aspects of life in America appealed to him. He found American society refreshingly different from the complicated manners and numerous obligations of the royal court in Paris. Little did Lafayette know that the American Congress and General George Washington had grown frustrated with the French military officers who had come to America to join the revolutionary cause. The French soldiers usually demanded extra privileges and generous pay. This caused resentment among the troops. Unfortunately, Congress practically slammed the door in the face of the expectant Lafayette. The young Frenchman was stunned.

Lafayette immediately sent a petition to Congress, volunteering to pay his own way and that of his staff. Congress ended up granting him an honorary position as major general. However, they did not intend to have him serve in action.

A few days later, Lafayette finally met the man who became his lifelong hero and mentor, General George Washington. Washington was 45; Lafayette was 19. Both were over six feet tall, and both lost their fathers at an early age. The two began a deep friendship.

Washington, a brilliant military leader, surrounded himself with his officers and aides and treated them like a family. He included younger officers in planning sessions as if they were trusted apprentices. One of Washington's aides was Alexander Hamilton, only a few months older than Lafayette. Hamilton and Lafayette also became friends.

Lafayette had an open, charming personality and showed respect to all. His enthusiasm and willingness to help impressed the Americans. He stated humbly to Washington, "I have come here to learn, not to teach." As a result, his fellow officers and the soldiers under him tended to respond warmly to Lafayette.

Lafayette Gains Fame in Battle

Within a few weeks, Washington invited Lafayette to attend a council of war. British troops had been sighted sailing south. Were they planning to attack Philadelphia?

Washington listened to the ideas of all his generals. For Lafayette, this was another difference from European tradition. In France, high-ranking military authorities did not usually ask the opinions of junior officers. Washington and his council decided that the British were probably heading for South Carolina. But they were mistaken. The British ships turned around and sailed toward Philadelphia.

On September 11, 1777, American troops defended the outskirts of Philadelphia. Unexpectedly, the British surrounded Washington's army. Upon hearing this news, Lafayette rode forward to help. He arrived just in time to see General Charles Cornwallis's troops attacking the American lines. The American defenses began to break down.

Lafayette jumped from his horse and shouted to restore an orderly defense, even grabbing men by their shoulders and turning them around. He didn't notice that he had been struck in the calf by a bullet. At last, the men responded to his attempts. They were impressed—a French officer had joined them on foot instead of remaining on horseback!

Lafayette showed great dexterity in guiding an orderly retreat. At one point, he blocked access to a bridge to force the soldiers to reform their lines.

After the battle, Washington had Lafayette taken to a nearby church to have his wounded leg cared for. There, Lafayette met a young captain, James Monroe—another future U.S. President who would become a lifelong friend.

Monroe had been wounded in a previous battle, and he kept Lafayette company. In conversation with the marquis, Monroe practiced his French, telling Lafayette about his mentor, Thomas Jefferson, author of the Declaration of Independence and yet another future U.S. President. The two young officers talked long into the night.

The day after the battle, General Washington praised Lafayette's courage and conduct in a report to John Hancock, president of Congress. It was Lafayette's first battle, and he had emerged a hero.

Not even two months later, his wound still healing, Lafayette eagerly returned to Washington's camp. He strongly wished to have an official leadership role. Washington wrote to Congress, recommending that Lafayette be given a division of troops.

While waiting for Congress to respond to Washington's letter, Lafayette accompanied General Nathaniel Greene to New Jersey. There, Greene assigned him 400 soldiers to lead.

Greene asked Lafayette to ride forward with his men and scout the positions of the nearby British troops. Lafayette eagerly attacked an outpost of General Cornwallis's army and drove it back a half-mile. He kept his soldiers in place till nightfall, establishing the skirmish as a victory.

Light Troops

The Marquis de Lafayette leads American troops into battle.

Americans made much use of light troops in the Revolutionary War. Light troops consisted of rapid-moving, specialized units such as riflemen and troops on horseback. These troops mostly operated from positions detached from the main army.

A light force had the advantage of great dexterity; it could attack an enemy in many ways. For example, light troops could harass the rear and sides of an enemy army from behind the shelter of trees and brush. While spread out, men could keep moving while firing shots from different locations. This tactic could make a small group of soldiers appear to be much larger.

The use of light troops helped the Americans achieve victory in the Revolutionary War. By employing light troops, engaging in tactical skirmishes, and avoiding head-on clashes, Washington and his generals eventually wore out the British forces.

The Marquis de Lafayette was skilled in commanding light troops in America. Later he helped expand their use in Europe.

A Division of His Own

After Lafayette's victory in New Jersey, Washington again requested that Congress give the marquis command of a division. In December 1777, Lafayette at last received his own division of more than 3,000 troops.

That winter at Valley Forge, the American army suffered through starvation, lack of clothing, frostbite, and illness. Lafayette could have bought a comfortable home nearby. He chose instead to live in difficult conditions among the soldiers. "The soldier's friend" spent his own money making sure his troops had basic supplies and provisions.

Lafayette proved his leadership and loyalty again and again to General Washington. He earned Washington's trust, obeyed him, and tried to make decisions like him.

The marquis continued to improve his battle skills. At Barren Hill, he and his division were nearly trapped by the British. Lafayette made a clever escape. He posted a few men to keep moving among the woods at night. This distracted the enemy's attention long enough for Lafayette to remove his troops from the trap.

General Washington and Lafayette at Valley Forge, 1777

Lafayette, the Diplomat

In 1778, the American revolutionaries received good news. Impressed by the colonists' recent victories against the British, France officially joined the war on the American side and declared its support for American independence.

Upon hearing the good news, Lafayette asked Washington for permission to return to France. The marquis felt that he could be of great help to the Americans through his connections and influence in France. Washington agreed, and Lafayette set sail for home.

When Lafayette arrived in France, King Louis XVI gave him a symbolic punishment. After all, the marquis had left to fight for the Americans without the king's permission. The punishment consisted of being confined to his family's palace. After a week's confinement, Lafayette's disobedience was officially forgiven, and he was welcomed at court.

At this same time, Benjamin Franklin and John Adams were in France, working to gain support, money, and supplies for the American cause. Lafayette met with Franklin and Adams, and the three men began to work together.

Lafayette quickly developed the skills of a successful diplomat. He met with the rich and powerful to promote the American cause. Lafayette kept up a barrage of suggestions to the French foreign ministers. He campaigned relentlessly for the French to send fleets of warships, thousands of troops, and loans to finance the war.

At last, Franklin, Adams, and Lafayette succeeded in their efforts, and the French government agreed to send generous financial and military aid to the Americans. Thanks to his firsthand knowledge of the American conflict and his many contacts at the French royal court, Lafayette played a key role in this diplomatic victory. He had become one of the most influential links between France and the American colonies.

French Salons

In 18th-century Paris, politics and society mixed at gatherings in the luxurious homes of French aristocrats. These gatherings were known as *salons*. Artists, writers, politicians, and others mingled at the salons. The Marquis de Lafayette was a significant figure in many Parisian salons.

Important foreigners were also welcome. American diplomats such as Benjamin Franklin, John Adams, and Thomas Jefferson regularly attended salons in order to meet powerful members of the French government and persuade them to support the American cause.

Years after the war ended, Lafayette and his wife hosted their own salon in Paris. Through this and other efforts, Lafayette continued to help his American friends.

Benjamin Franklin was a popular visitor at salons in Paris, France.

Victory at Yorktown

In the spring of 1780, once his diplomatic mission had succeeded, Lafayette returned to America, where the war continued. Washington welcomed him back and gave Lafayette command of another light division.

As usual, Lafayette spent his own money to outfit his troops. He also worked nonstop to get supplies for the starving American army. He and Alexander Hamilton wrote endless requests to Congress, colonial authorities, and French leaders, badgering anyone and everyone for provisions, clothing, arms, and supplies.

Meanwhile, British troops under the command of General Cornwallis were marching from South Carolina to Virginia. Their plan was to attack the city of Richmond, the capital of the colony.

In response to Cornwallis's movement, Washington assigned Lafayette a small detachment of light troops and sent them to Virginia. On his arrival, Lafayette was given command of additional American troops.

This historic map was drawn by one of Lafayette's aides.

General Cornwallis arrived in Virginia with an army of about 7,000 soldiers. In contrast, Lafayette had fewer than 1,000 soldiers. Washington instructed Lafayette to hold Cornwallis's army in Virginia, blocking its movements without engaging the more numerous British troops in battle. Lafayette's small force could not risk a major move against the enemy at that time. They had to wait for the arrival of a fleet of French warships.

Following Washington's instructions, Lafayette focused on staying near Cornwallis's troops. When Cornwallis marched his army inland to seize Richmond, Lafayette doggedly followed him. The British troops could not stay inland long, as Lafayette knew. Cornwallis and his army had to return to the coast because they depended on supplies from British ships docked there.

As Cornwallis moved his army back toward the coast, Lafayette and his forces shadowed the British, eventually trapping Cornwallis and his army on the peninsula at Yorktown. With this strategic move, the trap was set.

Meanwhile, Washington moved thousands of soldiers into Virginia. Then the long-awaited French fleet finally arrived, blocking sea access to Virginia. Suddenly surrounded by enemies on land and on the sea, Cornwallis realized that he had no escape route; he surrendered to the American forces at Yorktown in October 1781. Washington's and Lafayette's plan had worked, and the last great conflict of the American Revolution was won.

After the War

In 1784, after the Revolutionary War was won, Lafayette traveled around the new American nation. Although the individual states disagreed on almost everything, they all joined in gratefully honoring "our Marquis" for his role in winning their freedom.

Still a young man at the end of the Revolutionary War, Lafayette returned to his wife and family in France and stayed active in French politics. Nonetheless, his interest and involvement in the United States never faltered; for years after the American Revolution, Lafayette continued to help the United States gain recognition, trading privileges, and partnerships in Europe. He remained America's steadfast friend.

Decades later, that friendship was still strong. In 1824, President James Monroe, Lafayette's old comrade from the Revolutionary War, invited the marquis to visit the United States again and tour the country as the "Nation's Guest." Almost fifty years had passed

The Marquis de Lafayette as he looked during his tour of the U.S. in 1824

since Lafayette first set foot on American soil. But when the marquis arrived in America, adoring crowds turned out everywhere to greet and honor the beloved hero.

In 1834, when the marquis died at the age of 76, the entire American nation mourned the loss of one of the country's best friends and allies. Lafayette was buried in Paris alongside his wife, Adrienne. His grave was covered with American soil from the site of the Battle of Bunker Hill.

Epilogue

Today in the United States, Lafayette's many contributions to America's freedom have not been forgotten. In fact, his name can be seen everywhere. More than 600 American towns, parks, schools, counties, mountains, lakes and rivers, and other land-marks have been named in honor of the marquis. Princeton and Harvard universities granted him honorary degrees. And in 2002, Congress proclaimed the noble French patriot, Lafayette, a United States citizen.

The Life of the Marquis de Lafayette

September 6, 1757 • Gilbert du Motier, the future Marquis de Lafayette, is born in Auvergne, France.

1770 • Lafayette is orphaned, inherits his title, and becomes one of the richest men in France.

1774 • Lafayette enters military training.

1775–1776 • The American Revolutionary War begins.

April 20, 1777 • Lafayette leaves France to volunteer in the American army.

July 1777 • Congress commissions Lafayette as a major general.

August 1777 • Lafayette meets his future mentor and friend, George Washington.

September 1777 • Lafayette proves his abilities at the Battle of Brandywine near Philadelphia.

1778–1780 • Lafayette returns to France to seek French help as America's ally in the war. After his diplomatic success, he returns to America in spring 1780.

October 1781 • Lafayette plays a key role in Cornwallis's surrender at Yorktown.

1781–1783 • Lafayette returns to France and works to build U.S. trade in Europe.

1784 • Lafayette travels around the U.S. after the war.

1824–1825 • Lafayette tours the U.S. as the "Nation's Guest."

May 20, 1834 • Lafayette dies at the age of 76.

Responding

TARGET SKILL **Sequence of Events** What was the sequence of events that led Lafayette to fight on the side of the Patriots during the Revolutionary War? Copy and complete the chart below, adding boxes if necessary.

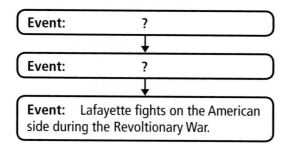

Event: ?

↓

Event: ?

↓

Event: Lafayette fights on the American side during the Revoltionary War.

Write About It

Text to World Lafayette showed great leadership ability during the Revolutionary War. Think of a modern figure who exhibits this quality. Write several paragraphs explaining what makes that person a great leader.

apprentice	dexterity
aspects	influential
authorities	persuade
bondage	provisions
contributions	tentative

EXPAND YOUR VOCABULARY

barrage	outpost
decoy	skirmish
infantry	tactical

✔ **TARGET SKILL** **Sequence of Events** Identify the time order in which events take place.

✔ **TARGET STRATEGY** **Summarize** Briefly tell the important parts of the text in your own words.

GENRE **Narrative Nonfiction** gives factual information by telling a true story.